UNLOCKING YOUR BRILLIANCE:
A Road Map Guide to
Unleashing your full Potential

Steven R. Amerson

TABLE OF CONTENTS

INTRODUCTION

In the boundless depths of the human spirit lies a treasure trove of untapped abilities, talents, and aspirations. This latent power, often concealed by self-doubt, external pressures, and the hustle of daily life, is what we refer to as "full potential." It's the hidden reservoir of capabilities that can lead you to unparalleled personal and professional growth, allowing you to achieve your dreams, make a meaningful impact, and live a life of purpose and fulfillment.

The journey of unleashing your full potential is a transformative one, where self-discovery, determination, and perseverance become your guiding stars. It's about breaking free from the constraints that have held you back, shedding the layers of self-limitation, and embarking on a voyage to uncover the greatness within.

This book is your compass on that transformative journey. It will delve into the core concepts of potential and guide you through the process of recognizing, nurturing, and ultimately maximizing your unique abilities. Along the way, you'll learn the tools and strategies that can help you become the best version of yourself.

By the end of this book, you will be equipped with the knowledge, insights, and inspiration needed to embrace your full potential and lead a life that harmonizes with your deepest aspirations. So, let's embark on this exhilarating voyage of self-discovery and personal growth, as we explore the incredible power of unleashing your full potential.

CHAPTER 1

DEFINITION AND EXPLANATION OF UNCOVERING YOUR FULL POTENTIAL

"Full Potential: *Unleashing Human Capacity*"

The concept of full potential is a deeply ingrained aspiration in human culture and self-improvement. It represents the idea of achieving the highest possible level of one's abilities, skills, and capabilities. It's the realization of the untapped reservoir of talent, intellect, and creativity that lies within each individual. Fulfilling one's full potential is a pursuit that transcends cultures, ages, and circumstances, and it continues to be a driving force for personal and collective progress.

Understanding Full Potential

Full potential is not a static, universally defined goal; rather, it's a highly personal and dynamic concept. It varies from person to person and evolves over time as individuals grow and develop. It encompasses multiple dimensions of life, including intellectual, emotional, physical, and social aspects. To better comprehend this multifaceted concept, we can break it down into a few key elements:

Self-Discovery: The journey toward full potential often begins with self-discovery. Understanding one's strengths, weaknesses, passions, and purpose lays the foundation for growth. This process involves introspection, self-reflection, and seeking feedback from mentors and peers.

Continuous Learning: Achieving full potential is an ongoing process. It involves a commitment to lifelong learning and personal growth. This may take the form of formal education, reading, skill development, and embracing new experiences.

Resilience: Facing challenges and setbacks is an integral part of the journey to full potential. Resilience, or the ability to bounce back from adversity, is crucial. It's about learning from failures, adapting to change, and persevering in the face of obstacles.

Passion and Purpose: Full potential is closely tied to pursuing one's passion and aligning one's actions with a sense of purpose. When individuals engage in activities they are deeply passionate about, they often find it easier to tap into their full potential.

Goal Setting: Clear goals act as milestones on the path to full potential. They provide direction, motivation, and a sense of accomplishment when achieved. Setting both short-term and long-term goals is essential.

Positive Mindset: A positive mindset plays a vital role in reaching one's full potential. Believing in one's abilities, cultivating a growth mindset, and maintaining a can-do attitude are essential components.

Well-Being: Physical and mental well-being are critical aspects of unlocking full potential. Taking care of one's health, managing stress, and ensuring a balanced lifestyle contribute to overall productivity and creativity.

Support Networks: No one reaches their full potential in isolation. Supportive relationships with family, friends, mentors, and colleagues can provide guidance, encouragement, and valuable feedback.

Adaptability: The world is constantly changing, and adaptability is crucial in realizing one's full potential. Being open to new ideas, technologies, and methodologies is essential for staying relevant and innovative.

Obstacles to Reaching Full Potential

Several obstacles can impede the journey toward one's full potential. These obstacles may include self-doubt, fear of failure, procrastination, lack of self-discipline, external pressures, and a fixed mindset. Overcoming these hurdles requires self-awareness, determination, and often, external support.

CHAPTER 2

IMPORTANCE OF FULFILLING FULL POTENTIAL

Why is self-awareness such a big deal?

Self-discovery is crucial because it makes life more purposeful. Knowing oneself better teaches you how to look for yourself. Plus, if you're honest to yourself, you could discover a more satisfying work. Additionally, your chances of success are higher if your job choice is one you are genuinely enthusiastic about.

Maybe you'll discover that, despite your introversion, you have a strong social skillset. Maintaining our social health is always crucial, but you could require more social interaction than you first thought.

This also helps you to better define your goals for the future. Knowing who you are will help you create a future that meets your requirements and promotes your well-being. You can't lead the most passionate and contented life without self-discovery.

Let's imagine you reflect a little and find that the projects you lead at work are your favorites. That most likely indicates that you are gifted or passionate about leadership. You may then work toward becoming a manager with that in mind.
You'll discover a position that you're more enthusiastic about and have a clearer career path.

You'll discover a position that you're more enthusiastic about and have a clearer career path.

Knowing oneself also allows you to identify your advantages and disadvantages. Perhaps you have a talent for compassion, empathy, or mindfulness. Alternatively, you can be a gifted writer or public speaker. The greatest approach to finding out is to start your path of self-discovery.

You may also identify where you need to grow with the aid of this procedure. You may see if you need to improve your communication abilities, for example, by reflecting on yourself.

Your self-discovery will influence other people's lives as well. With your newly honed abilities, you can build stronger bonds and engage socially. Being genuine will make you a better family member, friend, and employee.

Realizing one's full potential is not only personally fulfilling but also has broader implications. When individuals reach their full potential, they become valuable contributors to society, innovation, and progress. They are more likely to make meaningful contributions in their careers, communities, and fields of interest.

The quest to unlock one's full potential is a lifelong journey that involves self-discovery, continuous learning, resilience, and a positive mindset. It is a dynamic, personal endeavor that can lead to personal fulfillment and the betterment of society as a whole. As individuals strive to fulfill their potential, they contribute to a world that is enriched by their talents, creativity, and determination.

Personal Fulfillment: Achieving one's full potential leads to a sense of personal fulfillment and satisfaction. It can result in a deeper understanding of one's abilities and a greater sense of purpose and self-worth.

Higher Productivity: Individuals and organizations that operate at their full potential are more productive and efficient. They can accomplish more with fewer resources, leading to improved outcomes and greater success.

Innovation: Realizing full potential often involves pushing boundaries and thinking creatively. This drives innovation and progress, benefiting not only the individual or organization but also society as a whole.

Competitive Advantage: In a competitive world, those who reach their full potential gain a significant advantage. They are better equipped to excel in their chosen fields, outperform competitors, and adapt to changing environments.

Positive Impact: Individuals who fulfill their potential often make a positive impact on their communities and the world. They contribute to social, environmental, and humanitarian causes, thereby creating a better world for all.

Career Success: Realizing one's full potential can lead to career advancement and success. It can result in higher earning potential, job satisfaction, and recognition for one's achievements.

Personal Growth: The journey to full potential involves continuous learning and self-improvement. This leads to personal growth, expanded horizons, and a deeper understanding of oneself and the world.

Resilience: Those who have reached their full potential are often more resilient. They can adapt to challenges, bounce back from setbacks, and face adversity with confidence.

Motivation and Purpose: The pursuit of full potential provides individuals with a strong sense of motivation and purpose. It gives life direction and a reason to strive for excellence.

Role Model Effect: People who fulfill their potential can inspire and motivate others to do the same. They serve as role models, showing what can be achieved with determination and hard work.

In summary, realizing one's full potential is not only personally fulfilling but also beneficial to society and organizations. It leads to improved productivity, innovation, and personal growth, and it can have a positive impact on the world at large. As individuals and entities continually strive to reach their full potential, they contribute to a more prosperous and enlightened society.

CHAPTER 3

STRATEGIES FOR SELF-DISCOVERY

Self-discovery is a lifelong journey that involves gaining a deeper understanding of oneself, one's values, beliefs, strengths, weaknesses, and aspirations. It is a process that can lead to personal growth, increased self-awareness, and a stronger sense of purpose. To embark on this journey of self-discovery, one can employ various strategies and approaches. In this discussion, we'll explore several strategies for self-discovery in detail to provide a comprehensive perspective.

Life moves fast. We have work to do, errands to run, and obligations to fulfill. The last thing on our minds could be how to start a self-discovery journey.

We hardly ever have time in our hectic schedules to think about the type of life we genuinely want. While waiting in line at the grocery store, do you think about who you are? Probably not. Finding the time and space to explore and develop into our most true selves may be challenging. But several advantages make investing the effort worthwhile.

Committing is the first step in self-discovery, if you're wondering how to start. You will need to prioritize your needs, stay focused, and act along your journey. Recall that without effort, transformation is not possible.

Are you prepared to learn how to start your path of self-discovery? First, let's clarify what self-discovery is.

What is meant by self-discovery?
Understanding who you are—your beliefs, your needs and desires, even your likes and dislikes in food—is the process of self-discovery. Some of these self-discovery insights may have come to you organically over time. However, many of us have a tendency to lose sight of our moral compass and to keep our desires and impulses hidden—even from ourselves. Developing your self-discovery further can change your life.

It's one thing to know your personality type or your favorite meal. But true self-discovery starts when you evaluate your life and think about what's energizing and what's not. What will bring more joy into your life? What inspires you to jump out of bed each morning?

Once you've discovered more about yourself, you'll have an easier time finding your life purpose and being your authentic self in work as well as in your personal life. Understanding what's been missing from your life will help you learn about yourself.

But don't think you can finish this journey overnight. Self-discovery is an ongoing process. It requires you to dive in and examine all areas of your life and take the time to reflect. You'll need courage and resilience to stick with the process — in the process of looking inward, you may learn things about yourself that you find hard to accept.

Discovering your inner self also requires lots of self-awareness, otherwise known as self-knowledge. Self-knowledge usually refers to your knowledge of your feelings, beliefs, and desires. If you have more of this in your life, you'll have better emotional regulation. This will help you better your personal and work relationships and improve your stress management.

Knowing more about the way your mind works also improves your empathy, helps you exercise better exercise restraint, be more imaginative, and feel better about yourself. As a consequence, you'll even be more truthful.

Understanding how to begin a path of self-discovery has countless advantages. It is crucial to initiate action and make a start.

How to begin a journey of self-discovery
The idea of setting off on a self-discovery adventure may scare you. How how do you start? The path to self-discovery is not predetermined. This implies that you can begin with any activity that seems appropriate to you. Recall that starting this trip with bravery is already admirable, so maintain your momentum.

Here are 11 tips you can follow to learn how to discover yourself:

No matter what you're doing, strive to be your best self every single day.
Try new things and take chances.
Focus on your interests and what excites you.
Recognize your advantages and consider how you might use them elsewhere.
Write down your ideas in a diary so you may come back to them later.
Make sure the people in your life are encouraging to you. Take responsibility for your mistakes and move on.
Reconnect with your inner child by thinking back to your early years.
Ask inquiries and show curiosity.
Create behaviors that advance your goals and personal development.
Talk to yourself positively and give yourself rewards when you succeed.

Seven (7) components of self-discovery
Realizing who you are can boost your self-assurance in your ability to make decisions.

This applies to all aspects of your life as self-discovery fosters a profound understanding of who you are. Nobody else will be able to tell you what's best for you.

When striving to enhance your self-awareness, bear the following seven points in mind:

Consider your beginnings and your daily accomplishments.
Pay close attention to what energizes you and what depletes it.
Envision the individual you aspire to be.
Go with the flow of your interests and passions.
Let rid of your self-doubt and inner critic.
Make a meaningful life choice and behave with intention.
Take pride in your strength, fortitude, and fortitude in trying times.

other strategies for self-discovery are;

Journaling: Keeping a journal is a powerful tool for self-discovery. Writing down your thoughts, feelings, and experiences can help you gain insight into your emotions and thought patterns. Regular journaling allows you to track your personal growth and identify recurring themes in your life.

Self-Reflection: Take time to contemplate your experiences, actions, and decisions. Self-reflection can help you understand why you do the things you do and how your past has shaped your present. This can be done through meditation, mindfulness, or simply setting aside time for introspection.

Personality Assessments: Consider taking personality assessments like the Myers-Briggs Type Indicator (MBTI), the Enneagram, or the Big Five personality traits test. These assessments can provide valuable insights into your personality, preferences, and behaviors.

Seek Feedback: Ask for feedback from friends, family, and colleagues. Sometimes, others can offer valuable perspectives on your strengths and areas for improvement that you may not be aware of.

Explore Your Interests: Engage in a variety of activities and hobbies to discover what truly interests you. Exploring different interests can lead to the recognition of new passions and talents.

Set Goals: Define both short-term and long-term goals. Setting and achieving goals can help you understand what truly matters to you and what you are capable of.

Mentorship and Coaching: Seek guidance from mentors or coaches who can provide valuable insights and help you navigate your personal and professional development. No broaden your horizons and challenge your existing beliefs and perspectives. This exposure can be a catalyst for self-discovery.

Embrace Challenges: Don't shy away from challenges and adversity. Overcoming obstacles can reveal your resilience, determination, and problem-solving abilities.

Read Widely: Reading books, articles, and research on various subjects can expose you to new ideas and perspectives. This can spark self-discovery by challenging your existing beliefs and encouraging critical thinking.

Mind-Body Connection: Pay attention to the mind-body connection. Practices like yoga, meditation, and mindfulness can help you become more aware of the connection between your mental and physical well-being.

Face Your Fears: Confront your fears and step out of your comfort zone. It's often in moments of discomfort that you learn the most about yourself.

Counseling and Therapy: Professional counseling or therapy can provide a safe space to explore your thoughts, feelings, and past experiences in-depth. A trained therapist can help you navigate the process of self-discovery.

Document Your Values: Identify your core values and beliefs. Understanding what you stand for can guide your decisions and actions, leading to a more authentic life.

Connect with Nature: Spending time in nature can be a meditative and enlightening experience. It can help you reconnect with your inner self and gain a sense of peace and clarity.

Life Experiments: Experiment with different lifestyles or routines to see what aligns with your values and preferences. This might include trying minimalism, veganism, or other personal experiments.

Social and Emotional Intelligence: Develop your social and emotional intelligence by learning to understand and manage your emotions, as well as empathize with others. This can provide a deeper understanding of human nature and your own emotional responses.

Forgiveness and Letting Go: The process of forgiving and letting go of past grudges and regrets can be liberating. It allows you to move forward and discover your true potential.

Creativity and Art: Engaging in creative activities such as painting, writing, or music can be a way to express your inner thoughts and feelings, leading to self-discovery.

Connect with Others: Building meaningful relationships can help you discover different facets of yourself. Interactions with others can be mirrors reflecting your strengths and areas of growth.

Legacy and Contribution: Consider what kind of legacy you want to leave behind and how you can contribute positively to the world.

This can be a source of purpose and self-discovery.

In conclusion, self-discovery is a lifelong journey filled with twists and turns. It involves introspection, exploration, and growth. By employing these strategies and remaining open to change and new experiences, you can uncover your true self, discover your passions, and lead a more fulfilling life. Remember that self-discovery is not a destination but a continuous process of learning and evolving.

CHAPTER 4

NURTURING HIDDEN POTENTIAL

Nurturing hidden potential is a journey of self-discovery and personal growth. Many individuals possess untapped talents, abilities, and passions that, when uncovered and cultivated, can lead to a more fulfilling and successful life. In this discussion, we'll explore effective ways to nurture your hidden potential.

Everybody has hidden or untapped skills. We let ourselves be too easily defined, believing that we are limited to the things we have experience doing and are incapable of accomplishing anything else. Not only is this incorrect, but it's also a risky way of thinking that can keep us from taking chances, seizing new opportunities, and developing as people. It's a common misconception that ability comes naturally or that one must be "gifted" to succeed in a certain area. However, this is untrue. If they are willing to invest the time and energy, everyone has the potential to develop their talents and abilities. Here are some pointers for identifying and developing your hidden talents:

Dream, Explore, and Uncover Your Inner Talents

1) Consider the activities you find enjoyable. You likely have an innate affinity for something if you find yourself pulled to it regularly. Which topic or pastime piqued your interest as a child? In your dreams, what do you want to do? What causes you to become distracted when working on it? You can find your talents by following these hints.

2) Observe what brings you into the state of flow. Total immersion in a task is known as The

Flow. When we are in Flow, the outer world disappears and time seems to stop because we are so absorbed in what we are doing. We are performing at the highest level because we are fully focused. We feel alive and energized when we are in the Flow because we are in our element. We are now utilizing our latent skills in this stage.

3) Examine the qualities that others find admirable in you. Ask people to help you identify your abilities if you find it difficult. Those who know you the best are sometimes the ones who are better able to recognize your abilities than you are, find out what your coworkers, friends, and family believe are your strongest points. Give them your full attention and be receptive to their suggestions.

4) Think about anything you want to get better at. Examining the areas where you would like to make improvements might also help you discover your strengths. When you think there's space for improvement, what comes to mind first? Which talents are you interested in learning? Your desires can frequently be an indicator of untapped potential.

5) Go against the ideas that restrict you. Self-doubt is one of the largest barriers to realizing your latent skills. We let our limiting ideas and negative self-talk prevent us from achieving our goals much too frequently. If you catch yourself having self-doubt, consider the source of your belief. Which proofs do you have for that? After you have refuted your unfavorable views, you may begin to swap them out for powerful, positive ones.

6) Show openness to experimenting. Discovering your true interest requires experimenting with a variety of choices and situations. Taking risks and embracing new opportunities are two more benefits of trying new things. Stepping outside of your comfort zone is one of the finest methods to improve your abilities.

7) Trust your instincts. and the skull. After you've chosen a hobby or activity you're interested in, it's critical to conduct a study and confirm that you can picture yourself pursuing this endeavor in the long run. After you have a firm grasp of the responsibilities, you can begin to create a strategy for turning your talent into a reality.

8) Develop your abilities. You won't always be good at something just because you have a

natural passion for it. To develop your abilities and transform them into skills, you need patience, practice, and persistence. If you are dedicated to developing your skills, don't give up if you don't see results right away. If you persist at it and trust your gut, you will ultimately succeed.

9) Look for chances to put your skills to work. Finding chances to put your hidden skill to use is crucial when you've discovered it. Seek opportunities to put your writing gift to use if you have one. Perhaps you might write articles for a neighborhood magazine or launch a blog. If you have artistic skills, try to find opportunities to show off your creations to others.

10) Show patience. It takes time to discover and identify your hidden skills. If you don't notice

results right away, don't give up. Any skill must be developed via practice and patience. You will ultimately see the desired effects if you have patience and persevere.

Persevering in the Face of Adversity

Put in some grit. Reaching your objectives won't be simple. Keep your enthusiasm and dedication to your objectives high, and keep working toward them even when things get difficult. People with grit are more likely to succeed because their enthusiasm keeps them going and they resist giving up!

If you feel that your enthusiasm is waning, remind yourself of the reasons that fulfilling your potential and your original excitement for achieving your objectives are vital to you.

Consider the advantages of achieving your potential for both you and other people.

Remain patient and don't give up. Becoming a master in anything requires many hours of effort; reaching your full potential can require much more time. Although studies have lately called into question the validity of the "10,000-hour rule," it is still true that mastery cannot be attained without constant practice and effort. Consider the daily or weekly progress you make rather than just your ultimate objective.

Consider those who have overcome adversity and failure in the past, like Dr. Seuss or Henry Ford, to keep yourself from giving up. They both persevered and succeeded.

Remind yourself to be patient because reaching your full potential takes time, and the journey itself is more important than the destination. Try taking a break and getting some rest if you feel yourself getting too irritated or dejected. In the end, you could be more productive if you take time off rather than continuing to work at a lower level while experiencing burnout.

Combat fear. Refrain from obsessing over failure. "Failure" implies that a lack of success is unachievable and conveys information about your character. That is untrue. Rather, accept the notion that you are capable of learning from your errors. Several attempts are usually necessary for success. It may be on your twentieth attempt, or perhaps your hundredth, that you finally succeed.

What might go wrong if you make an effort yet are unable to reach your objective? The result of failure is probably not going to be all that horrible. What then is there to be concerned about? If you are scared about attempting but failing, remember that individuals often overestimate the amount of guilt they would feel after failing to reach a goal.

Take pride in your achievements. It's great that you are striving to improve yourself as a person. When things become hard, take a minute to celebrate your efforts and the strides you have made toward realizing your potential. By doing this, you will increase your chances of holding strong and enduring any difficult situations you come across along the way.

If you find it difficult to feel proud of your achievements, consider writing a letter to yourself in the form of a conversation. Assume your friend has been working as hard as you have. I assume you would be pleased with her?

You would most likely congratulate her on her excellent job and urge her to keep going. Why would you be any less kind to yourself?

Locate a social network. Family, friends, and other members of your social network contribute to your sense of well-being and belonging, which helps to mitigate the stress that might result from not being able to accomplish your goals.
Just like with colds, emotions may "catch" in humans. Be in the company of positive individuals who are pursuing their objectives. You'll "rub off" on their positivity and ambition.

Other ways of nurturing hidden talent are;
Self-Reflection: Begin by taking time for self-reflection. Think about your interests, passions, and the activities that bring you joy.

Ask yourself what you've always wanted to pursue but haven't yet.

Identify Your Strengths: Recognize your strengths and talents. What are you naturally good at? Sometimes, our potential is closely tied to our innate abilities.

Set Clear Goals: Define specific, achievable goals that relate to your potential. These goals should challenge you and motivate you to grow.

Overcome Fear and Doubt: Hidden potential is often buried under layers of fear and self-doubt. Confront these emotions and work on building self-confidence.

Lifelong Learning: Commit to continuous learning and personal development. Take courses, attend workshops, and read books that align with your interests and potential.

Expand Your Comfort Zone: Growth occurs outside of your comfort zone. Challenge yourself to try new things, even if they make you uncomfortable at first.

Seek Feedback: Reach out to mentors, teachers, or experts in your chosen field. They can provide guidance and valuable feedback to help you nurture your potential.

Practice Patience: Realizing your hidden potential may take time. Be patient and persistent in your efforts, and don't be discouraged by setbacks.

Build a Support Network: Surround yourself with people who support your goals and encourage your growth. A strong support system can provide motivation and accountability.

Develop a Growth Mindset: Cultivate a growth mindset, which means believing that your abilities and intelligence can be developed through effort and learning.

Embrace Failure: Understand that failure is a part of the journey. Each failure is a lesson that can bring you closer to reaching your potential.

Experiment and Explore: Be open to experimenting with various activities and interests. Sometimes, your hidden potential may be in an unexpected area.

Stay Curious: Cultivate curiosity. The more you explore and inquire, the more likely you are to uncover new areas of potential.

Time Management: Efficiently manage your time to balance your existing commitments with your pursuit of hidden potential.

Take Calculated Risks: Don't be afraid to take calculated risks in the pursuit of your passions. Sometimes, these risks lead to remarkable discoveries.

Passion Projects: Dedicate time to passion projects. Even if they aren't your primary source of income, they can be a fulfilling way to nurture your potential.

Network and Collaborate: Connect with like-minded individuals in your area of interest.

Collaboration can lead to valuable insights and opportunities.

Meditation and Mindfulness: Practicing meditation and mindfulness can help you stay focused and reduce stress, enabling you to nurture your potential more effectively.

Document Your Journey: Keep a journal to record your progress and experiences. Documenting your journey can provide clarity and help you track your development.

Celebrate Achievements: Acknowledge and celebrate your achievements, no matter how small. Recognizing your progress can be motivating.

Seek Inspiration: Draw inspiration from the success stories of others who have realized their hidden potential. Their journeys can offer valuable insights and motivation.

Stay Flexible: Be open to adjusting your path as you discover new aspects of your potential. Flexibility allows for personal growth and adaptation.

Self-Compassion: Treat yourself with kindness and self-compassion. Avoid harsh self-criticism, as it can hinder your journey.

Give Back: Sometimes, nurturing your hidden potential involves using your talents and passions to contribute positively to your community or a cause you care about.

Balance and Well-Being: Maintain a balance between nurturing your potential and taking care of your physical and mental well-being. Health and happiness are essential for growth.

In conclusion, nurturing hidden potential is a process that involves self-discovery, self-belief, and continuous effort. By implementing these strategies, you can uncover your latent talents and passions and develop them to their fullest potential. Remember that your potential is unique and may take various forms throughout your life. Embrace the journey, and with dedication and persistence, you can lead a more fulfilling and purpose-driven life.

CHAPTER 5

HOW TO IMPLEMENT YOUR FULL POTENTIAL

Realizing and implementing your full potential is a lifelong journey that involves self-awareness, personal growth, and consistent effort. It's about pushing your boundaries, pursuing your passions, and achieving your goals. In this extensive discussion, we'll explore a wide range of strategies and approaches to help you unlock your full potential, offering a comprehensive guide.

Self-Awareness: The first step in unlocking your potential is to understand yourself fully. This means recognizing your strengths, weaknesses, values, and passions. Self-awareness allows you to make choices that align with your true self.

Set Clear Goals: Clearly defined goals give you a sense of purpose and direction. Whether they're short-term or long-term, having goals helps you stay focused and motivated.

Continuous Learning: Commit to lifelong learning. Acquiring new knowledge and skills not only helps you adapt to a changing world but also expands your potential.

Embrace Failure: Don't fear failure; see it as an opportunity to learn and grow. Most successful people have faced setbacks but used them as stepping stones to reach their potential.

Resilience: Develop resilience to bounce back from adversity. It's a key trait in realizing potential, as life is filled with challenges.

Time Management: Efficiently manage your time by setting priorities, breaking tasks into smaller steps, and avoiding procrastination. This ensures you make the most of your time.

Mindfulness and Presence: Practice mindfulness to stay present in the moment. This helps you focus on the task at hand and make better decisions.

Network and Relationships: Build a strong network of friends, mentors, and colleagues. Your connections can open doors to new opportunities and provide valuable support.

Healthy Lifestyle: Take care of your physical and mental health. Regular exercise, a balanced diet, and adequate sleep are vital to maintaining the energy and focus needed to reach your potential.

Self-Confidence: Believe in yourself and your abilities. Self-confidence empowers you to take risks and push your limits.

Positive Thinking: Cultivate a positive mindset. Optimism can help you overcome challenges and see opportunities where others see obstacles.

Adaptability: Be flexible and open to change. The ability to adapt to different situations is essential in today's fast-paced world.

Passion and Purpose: Identify your passions and what gives your life meaning. Pursuing what you love can be a powerful motivator to reach your potential.

Mentorship: Seek guidance from experienced individuals who can provide insights and advice. Mentors can help you avoid common pitfalls and accelerate your growth.

Overcome Fear: Confront your fears and step outside your comfort zone. Many opportunities for growth are on the other side of fear.

Consistency: Consistency is key in achieving your potential. Regular, focused effort over time can yield significant results.

Set High Standards: Aim for excellence in everything you do. Raising your standards can push you to achieve more.

Creativity and Innovation: Foster creativity and innovation in your endeavors. Thinking outside the box can lead to breakthroughs and new opportunities.

Financial Literacy: Understand money and financial management. Financial stability is crucial in realizing your potential, as it provides you with the resources to invest in yourself and your goals.

Leadership Skills: Develop leadership skills, even if you're not in a formal leadership role. Leadership qualities like communication, decision-making, and teamwork are valuable in all aspects of life.

Emotional Intelligence: Enhance your emotional intelligence. Being in tune with your emotions and those of others can improve your relationships and decision-making.

Seek Feedback: Welcome constructive feedback from others. It can offer valuable insights and help you identify areas for improvement.

Visualize Success: Practice visualization by imagining your success in detail. This can boost your confidence and motivation.

Solve Problems: Develop problem-solving skills. Tackling challenges head-on and finding creative solutions is a fundamental aspect of realizing your potential.

Give Back: Contribute to your community or a cause you're passionate about. Helping others can be fulfilling and can also reveal hidden talents and potential.

Self-Discipline: Cultivate self-discipline to stay on track and resist distractions or temptations that may hinder your progress.

Keep a Growth Mindset: Embrace a growth mindset, where you believe that your abilities and intelligence can be developed through dedication and hard work.

Document Your Progress: Keep a record of your achievements and personal growth. Reflecting on your journey can be motivating and provide evidence of your potential realization.

Limit Negativity: Avoid toxic people and negative influences that can drain your energy and enthusiasm. Surround yourself with positivity and encouragement.

Accept Imperfection: Perfection is unattainable, and striving for it can hinder your progress. Embrace imperfection as a natural part of the growth process.

Stay Curious: Maintain a curious mindset. Asking questions and seeking new experiences can expand your horizons and unlock hidden potential.

Set Boundaries: Establish personal boundaries to protect your time and energy. This allows you to focus on what truly matters.

Celebrate Small Wins: Acknowledge and celebrate your small achievements along the way. This positive reinforcement can boost your motivation.

Lifelong Purpose: Continuously seek your purpose in life. Your potential can evolve as your understanding of your purpose grows.

In conclusion, unlocking your full potential is a continuous process that requires self-awareness, commitment, and a willingness to push your limits. It's not a destination but a journey filled with self-discovery and growth. By implementing these strategies and maintaining a growth mindset, you can realize your full potential and lead a more fulfilling life. Remember that your potential is limitless, and it's up to you to explore it to the fullest.

CHAPTER 6

OVERCOMING FEAR AND DOUBT

Overcoming fear and doubt is a crucial aspect of personal growth and success. These emotions can be powerful inhibitors, preventing you from pursuing your dreams and reaching your full potential. In this discussion, we'll explore effective strategies to conquer fear and doubt, offer comprehensive guidance.

Everybody experiences anxiety and doubt at some time in their travels. Several things might prevent us from reaching our objectives, including fear of failing, fear of the unknown, fear of taking chances, and self-doubt. But it's crucial to keep in mind that uncertainty and dread are normal feelings that everyone experiences. The secret is to develop the ability to overcome these obstacles and turn them into motivation to succeed.

It's acceptable to have fear or uncertainty, but you shouldn't let these emotions prevent you from going for your goals. We'll talk about some useful strategies in this blog article to help you get over uncertainty and anxiety and accomplish your goals as an entrepreneur.

Recognize Your Doubts and Fears

To overcome fear and uncertainty, you must first determine what is preventing you from moving forward. Give your thoughts and emotions some time to settle. What fears do you have? What uncertainties do you have regarding your skills?

Put your worries and anxieties in writing, being as detailed as you can. Consider why you are terrified of failing, for instance. Is it a result of your concern about other people's opinions? Or do you fear squandering cash and time?

It's simpler to face your worries and concerns head-on after you've recognized them. Make a strategy to deal with them and break them down into smaller, more doable actions. Never forget that it's OK to ask for assistance or guidance from those who have experienced comparable circumstances.

Change your mindset

Our capacity to overcome uncertainty and fear is greatly influenced by our mentality. Try to reframe feelings of uncertainty and worry as chances for development and education rather than as unpleasant feelings.

Accept the notion that failing is only a necessary step on the path to achievement rather than the conclusion. A lot of successful business owners have experienced several failures before reaching their objectives. Everything is a part of the process.

Concentrating on the advantages of reaching your objectives is another strategy for altering your perspective. Imagine what success looks like and the advantages it will bring to you and the people in your vicinity. This may inspire you to face the difficulties head-on and get over your uncertainties and worries.

Take Action

Taking action is one of the best strategies to get over feelings of uncertainty and dread. It's simple to fall into a loop of excessive overthinking and scenario analysis. But this may also result in passivity and procrastination.

Rather, concentrate on making tiny, gradual progress toward your objectives. Sort your projects according to significance and divide them into manageable portions. This might support your motivation and attention span.

Recall that progress takes precedence over perfection. Take risks and make mistakes without fear. You get closer to your objectives with every step you take, no matter how tiny.

Recall that success is a journey rather than a destination. Accept the highs and lows, grow from your errors, and continue forth. You can do everything you set your mind to if you have endurance and dedication.

TRANSFORMATION HATES IN YOUR BRAIN

It should come as no surprise that you will need to develop if you are on the path to becoming the best version of yourself.

It will be necessary for you to step outside of your comfort zone.

You'll need to let go of your previous routines and perspectives.

You will also need to adopt new viewpoints, acquire new concepts, and do bold, unsettling acts.

Fear is the one thing that cannot be avoided, which makes all of this much easier said than done.

Fear is a defense mechanism designed to keep you secure and at ease. This becomes an issue when you need to continuously push yourself to explore uncharted areas to bring about change and advancement to become the most successful version of yourself.

Fear may undermine you at every step if you never understand how important it is to your development and success.

However, you may utilize fear as fuel to create more development and transformation than ever before if you can learn to deliberately modify the way you relate to it.

Fear is the primary cause of the great majority of mental and emotional stress that we experience daily.

The primitive feeling of dread tries to prevent us from bravely coming forth as our greatest, most powerful selves, whether it's uncertainty, unworthiness, not wanting to fail, or not wanting to be judged.

The strange thing is, our brain believes that by holding us back with fear, it is doing us a favor.

During our prehistoric era, when there was always danger around, our overly protective fear response kept us alive. But actual threats were commonplace back then, every day.

Though fear is very firmly embedded in our minds, the dangers that fear was intended to protect us against aren't that much of an issue.

AN OVERLY PROTECTIONIST SOLDIER

But terror requires an opponent to keep us safe, much like an elderly soldier who has only experienced combat. Furthermore, it overreacts to our everyday lives in an attempt to fulfill its objective because there aren't many genuine threats hiding around every corner.

Additionally, uncertainty is the one thing that fear tries to "protect" you from the most.

The brain will produce a wide range of feelings (anxiety, uncertainty, concern, negativity, etc.) to discourage you from taking actions that have an uncertain result since it understands that novel and unfamiliar circumstances present the greatest harm.

That's why it may be so challenging to break old habits and form new ones.

Even if something doesn't serve us and advance us toward our objectives, our brains will do all in their power to protect us by clinging to what is most familiar.

Fear might be your deadliest adversary if you need to transform into a better, stronger, more competent version of yourself to reach your full potential and succeed.

TEARING DOWN FEAR AND GOING AHEAD

There is no easy method to overcome fear since it is a deeply rooted survival strategy that is closely nested inside the human mind.

Furthermore, fear will save you in an emergency where you may otherwise have to run for your life or battle a bear.

However, you may break free from fear's oppressive hold on you by altering your relationship with it.

Flexing your awareness muscle should be your initial step.
As soon as fear, or any of its allies, such as doubt, impostor syndrome, judgment, anxiety, etc., sets in, make it your goal to objectively recognize it as soon as you can.

Just admit that you are afraid without passing judgment on the circumstance or yourself.

Then, even though it may sound strange, give it thanks for attempting to keep you safe. Fear believes it is just keeping an eye on you, so be grateful and give credit where credit is due.

Next, exercise your reasoning skills and solve the situation.

When fear arises, it is a reaction to anything that threatens your security and well-being.

You can take action despite your fear if you can evaluate the situation and determine that the real threat is not to your physical health but rather to your old habits or beliefs. In this case, your fear is completely unfounded (if there is a pack of wolves, however, your need to flee is justified).

ENERGY AND OPERATIONS

This is the issue. At first, this sequence will seem quite weird.

It will take some work to pick up this new behavior pattern because we are conditioned to strictly follow our brains' instructions.

However, like with any new skill, it becomes more fluid with practice.

It gets easier to act boldly in the face of uncertainty the more you put this sequence into practice.

And you get momentum and strength when you can do that regularly.

On your route to greatness, you may conquer greater and scarier hurdles the better your talent gets and the more momentum you build up.

Acknowledge Your Fear and Doubt: The first step in overcoming fear and doubt is to recognize and accept that you are experiencing these emotions. Denying or suppressing them can be counterproductive.

Understand the Root Causes: Delve into the underlying reasons for your fear and doubt. Are they based on past experiences, self-criticism, or external influences? Understanding the source can help you address these emotions more effectively.

Positive Self-Talk: Replace negative self-talk with positive affirmations. Challenge your self-doubt by reminding yourself of your strengths and past achievements.

Visualize Success: Use the power of visualization to imagine yourself succeeding in your endeavors. Visualizing positive outcomes can boost your confidence and reduce fear.

Set Realistic Goals: Break down your goals into smaller, manageable steps. This makes the path to success less intimidating and allows you to build confidence as you achieve each step.

Embrace Failure as Learning: See failure as a stepping stone, not a roadblock. Every setback is an opportunity to learn and grow. Thomas Edison famously said, "I have not failed. I've just found 10,000 ways that won't work."

Learn from Role Models: Study the lives of individuals who have overcome fear and doubt to achieve remarkable success. Their stories can inspire and provide guidance.

Seek Support: Share your fears and doubts with friends, family, or a mentor. Sometimes, discussing your concerns with someone you trust can provide valuable perspective and encouragement.

Challenge Comfort Zones: Push yourself beyond your comfort zones. Growth often happens when you step into the unknown. As you do this, you'll discover that your comfort zone expands.

Mindfulness and Meditation: Mindfulness practices can help you stay present and calm in the face of fear and doubt. Meditation can reduce anxiety and increase your self-awareness.

Foster Resilience: Cultivate resilience by adapting to adversity. Resilient individuals bounce back from setbacks and use them as fuel for further progress.

Educate Yourself: Knowledge can be a powerful tool in combating doubt. The more you know about a subject or situation, the more confident you'll feel.

Celebrate Small Wins: Don't underestimate the importance of celebrating even the smallest achievements. Recognizing your progress can boost your confidence.

Stay Committed: Commitment to your goals and dreams is essential. Consistency and perseverance are often the keys to overcoming fear and doubt.

Conquer Perfectionism: Understand that perfection is unattainable. Set realistic standards for yourself and don't let the quest for perfection paralyze you.

Visualize Worst-Case Scenarios: Sometimes, the fear of the unknown is worse than the reality. Visualizing the worst-case scenario can help you realize it's not as bad as you imagined.

Time Management: Effective time management can reduce stress and prevent procrastination, which often stems from fear and doubt.

Take Breaks and Practice Self-Care: Burnout can intensify fear and doubt. Take regular breaks, practice self-care, and recharge your energy.

Professional Help: If your fear and doubt are paralyzing or deeply rooted, consider seeking professional help, such as therapy or counseling, to address and manage these emotions effectively.

Learn from Mistakes: Mistakes are part of the journey. Rather than dwelling on them, analyze what went wrong and use the lessons to improve.

Accept Imperfection: Embrace the idea that you don't have to be perfect to succeed. Embrace your flaws and see them as part of what makes you unique.

Maintain Perspective: Maintain a balanced perspective on your goals. Avoid making them the sole source of your self-worth.

Empowerment Through Knowledge: Remember that knowledge is empowering. The more you understand and prepare, the more you'll be able to confront your fears.

Release Control: Understand that you can't control everything. Embrace uncertainty and let go of the need for absolute control.

Practice Gratitude: Focusing on the positive aspects of your life can shift your mindset away from fear and doubt.

Surround Yourself with Positivity: Spend time with positive, supportive people who believe in your potential.

Realistic Expectations: Set realistic expectations for yourself. Recognize that progress may be slow, but it's still progress.

Self-Compassion: Be kind to yourself. Don't be too harsh or critical. Treat yourself with the same compassion you would offer a friend.

Journaling: Write down your fears and doubts. Analyzing them on paper can often lead to insights and solutions.

In conclusion, overcoming fear and doubt is a challenging but rewarding endeavor. It requires self-awareness, resilience, and a commitment to personal growth. By implementing these strategies, you can not only conquer your fears and doubts but also unlock your full potential, paving the way for a more fulfilling and successful life. Remember that everyone experiences fear and doubt at some point; the key is how you choose to confront and conquer them.

CHAPTER 7

CREATIVITY AND INNOVATION

Creativity and innovation are powerful catalysts that can significantly contribute to reaching one's full potential. They enable individuals to break through limitations, explore new possibilities, and achieve personal and professional growth in various ways. Here are several ways in which creativity and innovation can help individuals reach their full potential:

Innovation and creativity are critical abilities in the fast-paced world of today. They are essential in practically every industry, including business, science, technology, and design; they are not solely used by artists and designers. You may get a competitive advantage and make a statement by being imaginative and inventive.

We'll look at seven methods in this article to help you become more innovative and creative.

Remain open-minded: Remaining open-minded is among the most crucial things to accomplish. Your next brilliant idea might come from anywhere at any time. Keep an open mind to fresh concepts, viewpoints, and encounters. Read broadly to discover new subjects. Participate in events, make connections with individuals in other businesses, and take risks. Maintaining an open mind will enable you to generate fresh thoughts and view things from a different angle.

Engage in brainstorming: It's a straightforward yet effective way to come up with ideas. In a short period, a significant number of ideas must be generated. To begin, identify the issue or challenge that has to be resolved. Next, jot down as many concepts as you can, regardless of how sensible or doable they appear to be. After you've compiled a list of ideas, go over and improve each one to determine which is best.

Work together: Working together might help you come up with fresh concepts and see things from different angles. Working with individuals from other businesses and backgrounds might open your eyes to fresh perspectives.

Finding your ideas' gaps and blind spots might also be aided by working with others.

Try new things and take chances: Being creative requires a willingness to try new things and take chances. Don't be afraid to try new things, even if they appear strange or uncomfortable. It's okay to fail; it's all part of the learning process. You're more likely to come up with novel ideas and solutions the more experiments you conduct.

Allocate time for imaginative thought: Making time specifically for creative thought can aid in concentration and idea generation. This may be as easy as blocking out time on your schedule or designating a certain area for creative thought. You may improve your creative abilities over time by developing a habit of it.

Make use of technology: It may be an effective instrument for creativity and innovation. Utilize applications, software, and other resources to assist in idea organization, brainstorming, and teamwork. There are many tools out there that may help you come up with fresh ideas and organize your workflow.

Lastly, never stop learning and developing. Keep learning and improving. There is always something new to learn, and the world is ever-changing. Take classes, read books, and participate in seminars on subjects you find interesting. You can stay up to date with the newest concepts and trends and keep improving your creative and innovative abilities by always learning and developing.

Being innovative and creative are critical abilities that will make you stand out in the modern world. Your creativity and innovation skills can be developed and your full potential can be realized by keeping an open mind, practicing brainstorming, working with others, experimenting and taking risks, scheduling time for creative thinking, utilizing technology to your advantage, and never stopping learning and growing.

Problem Solving: Creative thinking and innovation can provide novel solutions to complex problems. When you can effectively solve challenges, you pave the way for personal and professional advancement.

Adaptability: Creativity and innovation foster adaptability. In a rapidly changing world, the ability to adapt to new situations and environments is crucial for realizing your full potential.

Unique Pathways: They allow you to carve out unique pathways to success. Instead of following conventional routes, creative thinking often leads to the discovery of unconventional, more efficient, and effective ways to achieve goals.

Continuous Learning: Creativity encourages a mindset of continuous learning. When you're open to new ideas and approaches, you are more likely to seek knowledge and grow throughout your life.

Enhanced Problem-Solving Skills: Creative thinking sharpens problem-solving skills, making you more adept at tackling obstacles and overcoming challenges that may have previously hindered your progress.

Innovation in Career: Innovation can lead to advancements in your career. It can help you discover fresh ways to excel in your field, possibly resulting in promotions, new opportunities, or the launch of your own ventures.

Expanded Horizons: Creativity and innovation open up new horizons, expanding your perspective and helping you see the bigger picture. This broader view can lead to more significant achievements and personal growth.

Fulfillment: Pursuing creative endeavors often leads to a sense of fulfillment and purpose. When you're passionate about your work, you're more likely to reach your full potential.

Confidence Building: Successful creative projects or innovative solutions can boost your self-confidence, enabling you to take on more significant challenges and believe in your abilities.

Resourcefulness: Creativity fosters resourcefulness. It helps you find innovative ways to make the most of your resources, which can be especially beneficial when pursuing ambitious goals.

Critical Thinking: Creative and innovative thinking encourages critical thinking. You become more skilled at analyzing situations, making informed decisions, and taking calculated risks.

Leadership Qualities: Creativity and innovation often lead to the development of leadership qualities. Creative individuals are often seen as visionary and capable of inspiring and leading others toward achieving their potential.

Positive Impact: Innovations often have a positive impact on the world, whether through new technologies, processes, or solutions.

Contributing to positive change can be an important part of reaching your full potential.

Adventurous Spirit: Creativity and innovation encourage an adventurous spirit. By embracing new challenges and risks, you gain the confidence to venture into the unknown, where hidden potential may be discovered.

Enhanced Communication: Creativity improves communication skills. Effective communication is essential for building relationships, networking, and sharing your ideas with others, which can be key to your growth and success.

Breaking Boundaries: Creative and innovative individuals are often boundary-breakers. They challenge traditional norms and pave the way for new paradigms and ways of thinking.

Resilience: Creativity and innovation can make you more resilient. When you're open to change and adaptation, you can bounce back from setbacks and stay committed to your goals.

Competitive Advantage: In competitive environments, creative thinking and innovation provide a competitive advantage, increasing your chances of achieving your potential.

In summary, creativity and innovation are integral to realizing one's full potential. They foster problem-solving, adaptability, and resourcefulness, enabling you to overcome challenges and make significant progress in your personal and professional life. By embracing creative thinking and innovative approaches, you can unlock new opportunities and achieve your full potential.

CHAPTER 8

ADVANTAGES OF TAPPING INTO YOUR FULL POTENTIAL

Tapping into your full potential offers a wide range of advantages that can positively impact various aspects of your life. When you harness your capabilities and utilize them to the fullest, you can achieve personal growth, success, and fulfillment. Here are some of the key advantages of realizing your full potential:

Personal Growth: Unlocking your full potential allows you to explore your abilities, skills, and talents, leading to significant personal growth. You continually evolve, learn, and adapt, becoming a better version of yourself.

Increased Self-Confidence: As you achieve your goals and overcome challenges, your self-confidence grows. This increased self-assurance empowers you to take on new opportunities and face adversity with resilience.

Achieving Goals: Your full potential enables you to set and accomplish ambitious goals. With focused effort, you can reach heights you might not have previously thought possible.

Career Advancement: In the professional realm, tapping into your full potential can lead to career advancement. It often results in better job opportunities, promotions, and increased earning potential.

Financial Stability: Realizing your full potential may open doors to higher-paying careers or entrepreneurial endeavors, ultimately leading to greater financial stability and security.

Improved Relationships: Personal growth often positively impacts your relationships. You become more empathetic, understanding, and effective in your interactions with others.

Enhanced Problem-Solving: Your full potential can make you a more effective problem solver. You can approach challenges with a creative and adaptable mindset, finding innovative solutions.

Higher Resilience: Tapping into your potential equips you with the resilience to bounce back from setbacks. You view failures as opportunities for growth rather than as insurmountable obstacles.

Greater Influence: As you achieve your potential, you become a source of inspiration and influence for others. Your success can motivate and guide those around you.

Sense of Fulfillment: Fulfilling your potential is deeply rewarding and provides a profound sense of fulfillment. You feel a greater purpose and satisfaction in your life.

Increased Productivity: Realizing your full potential often leads to increased productivity. You become more efficient and effective in your endeavors, allowing you to accomplish more in less time.

Better Health and Well-Being: Personal growth and achieving your potential can lead to better health practices. You're more likely to prioritize self-care, such as exercise, proper nutrition, and stress management.

Emotional Intelligence: Tapping into your potential enhances your emotional intelligence, allowing you to better understand and manage your emotions and those of others.

Stronger Decision-Making: With personal growth comes improved decision-making. You're more capable of making sound choices and weighing the pros and cons of different options.

Creativity and Innovation: Realizing your potential often unleashes creativity and innovation. You're more likely to think outside the box, develop new ideas, and contribute to positive change.

Legacy and Contribution: Achieving your potential allows you to leave a meaningful legacy and contribute positively to your community and the world.

Happiness and Life Satisfaction: Ultimately, realizing your full potential can lead to a higher overall level of happiness and life satisfaction. You're content with your accomplishments and the journey you've taken.

Adaptability: As you grow and tap into your potential, you become more adaptable to change and open to new experiences, which is valuable in a rapidly evolving world.

Positive Impact on Society: Your efforts to realize your potential can have a ripple effect, positively influencing your community and society at large.

A Sense of Control: Realizing your potential can provide a sense of control over your life and destiny. You become the author of your own story.

In summary, tapping into your full potential offers numerous advantages, both personally and professionally. It leads to personal growth, career success, increased confidence, and a greater sense of fulfillment. Ultimately, it enables you to make a positive impact on your own life and the lives of those around you, contributing to a better and brighter future.

www.ingramcontent.com/pod-product-compliance
Lightning Source LLC
Chambersburg PA
CBHW060943260726
48661CB00005B/1744